NOW!

NOW!

The Art of Being Truly Present

Jean Smith

Wisdom Publications • Boston

Wisdom Publications
199 Elm Street
Somerville, MA 02144 USA
www.wisdompubs.org

First Edition
09 08 07 06 05 04
6   5   4   3   2   1

Library of Congress Cataloging-in-Publication Data
Smith, Jean, 1938–
  Now! : the art of being truly present / Jean Smith.
     p. cm.
  Includes index.
  ISBN 0-86171-480-6 (pbk. : alk. paper)
  1. God—Attributes. I. Title.
  BL624.S5947 2004
  204'.32—dc22

                              2004006406

Wisdom Publications' books are printed on acid-free paper and meet the guidelines
for the permanence and durability set by the Council of Library Resources.

Cover design by Laura Shaw
Interior design by Gopa & Ted2. Set in Charlotte Sans 9.75/14 and Calligraph 18/28.

Printed in Canada.

For my sister, M' Liss

CONTENTS

Presence in the World

PREFACE

I WROTE *NOW! The Art of Being Truly Present* out of personal and national grief. Painful occurrences deluged my life in quick succession: the deaths of friends in the World Trade Towers, of a parent, and of a favorite pet. Each loss hurt as an arrow shot into me—and then I did my own mental version of time travel and began telling myself stories about my suffering, which felt like shooting a second arrow into the original wounds. With my internal monologues, I leapt out of the present moment and bared my heart to repeated piercing from the past.

To help break this cycle of suffering, I began using the reflections and invocations now compiled in this book to complement my traditional meditation practice. These practices together reined me back into the now, and I was able to confirm once again that being truly present with a clear mind and open heart can bring peace. I sincerely hope that you too will know renewed peace in the present.

Jean Smith
Taos, New Mexico
Fall 2004

INTRODUCTION

ONE FAMOUS AUTHOR AND SPIRITUAL TEACHER, Jack Kornfield, likes to quote a sign he saw in a Las Vegas casino: "You must be present to win." And Woody Allen has quipped, "About 80 percent of life is just showing up." Showing up in the present moment sounds simple—and it is—but it is not always easy. We are so used to leading laminated lives that we spend a great deal of time mindlessly, mechanically, on automatic pilot. But when we think of moments when we have really been here—for a beautiful sunset, a spectacular meal, a loving embrace, an extraordinary musical performance—we know what it means "to be present to win," and we know that it is possible for us. The door to the present moment, to true appreciation of our entire lives, is cultivation of the practice of mindful awareness, or mindfulness: consciously undertaking, with clear mind and open heart, an intimate relationship with the present.

Unfortunately, we do not come equipped with a mindfulness switch that we can simply turn on at will. In fact, we can only cultivate it with unambiguous intention and patience, continually resisting the momentum of cultural conditioning experienced from birth on that defies mindful awareness. Even as children we are taught that life is a competitive sport rather than a collaborative one, and we're pressed to be human havings and doings rather than human beings.

In the face of the cultural diversions that tug at humans to succeed, to accumulate, to strive for future goals, why have spiritual seekers for thousands of years cultivated mindfulness, and why should we? The simple answer is that we all want to be happy and that an enduring happiness is possible only by living fully in the reality of the *now*.

Mindfulness underlies all insightful living. We cannot have contented lives if we unthinkingly say and do things that cause others—and ultimately ourselves—suffering. Mindfulness is not itself a religion and yet is compatible with many. Through mindfulness, we become aware of the deep interconnection among all beings by recognizing that we all seek happiness even when our efforts are unskillful. We come to see clearly the immutable relationship between cause and effect and realize that nothing—no energy, no action, no intention—is ever lost. We recognize the presence of grace in our life. And we come to know the possibility of personal transformation. Although we cannot change our past, if we are truly and realistically mindful in the present, we come to know that the way we interact with the present will shape our future.

HOW TO USE THIS BOOK: COMING INTO THE PRESENT

Each selection, extending across facing pages, is devoted to a theme that is an integral aspect of daily living. These selections can be used for reflection, discussion in small groups, or journaling. You may choose to work with one topic for a day or for a week or longer. It is important no matter what approach you take that you take time to really answer for yourself two questions: *What does this have to do with me?* and *How can I make use of this?* It is helpful to use the selections for reflection in combination with a brief period of meditation, discussed below, either before or after. To explain how you can use the selections, we'll consider the example of anger, an all-too-common aspect of life.

When you read the title—"Anger"—pause for a few moments and ask yourself what associations the topic immediately brings up for you. Is anger a common emotion for you? What most often triggers anger in you? Are you comfortable with your own anger? With that of others? Is anger ever justified?

On the left-hand page, below the title, are several anecdotal statements about common experiences with the topic. To make the subject your own, try to come up with concrete examples of the expression of anger in your life or translate these anecdotes into your own experiences. Look for any common threads running through the experiences you reflect on.

When you feel you have touched your real experience of the topic, look at the short invocation on the right-hand page. The use of invocations, hymns, and verses as an aid for spiritual practice is found in nearly all traditions—Christianity, Judaism, Buddhism, Islam, Hinduism, and many Native American religions. The invocations here are perhaps closest to *gathas*, the name given to verses for reflection in the Buddhist tradition. You may wish just to read the verse you're involved with slowly and thoughtfully. You may wish to write it down and post it on your computer monitor or refrigerator as a reminder. Or you may want to memorize it and consciously bring it to mind during the day or week.

The effect of working through the selections this way is cumulative. You will gradually become aware that you are increasingly bringing mindfulness to new areas of your daily life. You will find many experiences start to transform in subtle and overt ways: music will seem more beautiful, affection will come to be more heartfelt, and most important of all, you will start to see a real connection with all beings and naturally will become a more generous member of your community and your world. You will know a new peace and contentment—because you'll really be present for your life.

MEDITATION PRACTICE

As mentioned above, the selections in this book are most effective when used in combination with some kind of meditation, because meditation is an exceptionally powerful practice for being in the present. If you do not already meditate, you can undertake a very simple practice: Each day, set aside a time and place where you can pause uninterrupted for a few minutes. Sit alertly (but not rigidly) in a chair or cross-legged on the floor. Do a brief scan of your body and try to relax any areas where you feel tension. Let your eyes close gently, and bring your attention to the one place where you most clearly feel your breath (usually nostrils, chest, or abdomen). Don't attempt to control or change your breathe—simply observe it, noting *inbreath* when you breathe in, and *outbreath* when you breath out. When your mind wanders—as everyone's surely will—very gently and without self-judgment bring your attention back to your breath as soon as you realize you've become lost in thoughts. Don't program yourself to failure by setting a goal of many minutes or an hour in the beginning. Start with just five or even three minutes, then increase the time later if you wish.

Even a few minutes in quiet meditation can calm your mind and open your heart, bringing you more deeply into the moment. And then, from that place, you can more effectively assimilate the reflections in this book and gradually transform your life into the life you most deeply want to it be.

PRESENCE
OF SPIRIT

FAITH

Everything will turn out the way it's supposed to.

Our relationship is based on mutual trust.

I have confidence in my doctor's plan for treatment
because I trust her.

WHENEVER WE EMBRACE FAITH or take an action on faith, we open ourselves to the great unknown. We are able to act "in good faith" because we trust that a spiritual belief, an ideal, or a person warrants our reliance. But we don't have to act on the basis of blind faith or blind trust. When we come fully into the present, we find evidence all around us for everything we would believe, trust, and have faith in.

May I be graced
with the power of a faith
that dispels doubt,
so that I can open to life's
mysteries and joys
with confidence.

MINDFUL AWARENESS

I didn't realize I was so angry until I blew up when he teased me.

I was so busy thinking about how I would describe my vacation,
I really didn't experience some of it.

I bought everything at the grocery store except what I went in for.

SO MUCH OF THE TIME, we are on automatic pilot, moving through our lives mechanically. Not mindfully aware in the moment, we miss out on our own lives and unconsciously do and say things that hurt others because we are reacting rather than responding appropriately to circumstances. Mindful awareness does not just happen—it must be cultivated through meditation or other spiritual practices. Only when we are mindful can we seize opportunities for conscious choices, act with kindness, and avoid hurting others through our actions and words.

May I cultivate mindful awareness
so that I may be fully present
for the spiritual life possible
only by dwelling in the now.

THE PRESENT MOMENT

I get terrible "performance anxiety" every time I know I will have to speak in public.

When I haven't visited my family during holidays, I've felt so guilty afterward.

I had painstakingly prepared the meal, but I was so busy talking I didn't even notice the food.

WHENEVER WE ARE EXPERIENCING FEAR, anxiety, or even strong desire, we are not in the present moment: We are worried about something that *will* happen in the future, or we are longing for something we do not have now. Caught up in guilt, remorse, or desire, we may completely miss what is happening in our world now. But even without such strong emotional pulls to future or past, we often aren't consciously in the present, and we miss many of the blessings here for us. There is nothing wrong with planning or remembering, but the only reality—the only opportunity where true choice exists, where genuine happiness can be felt—is the present moment.

May I infuse my life
with mindful attention,
moment by moment,
so that I may live
with the love, happiness,
and choices
that I can only know in the now.

MINDFULNESS BELLS

My doorbell rings.

The kitchen timer goes off.

A clock chimes in my living room.

I hear dogs barking late at night.

A car horn blares outside my window.

EVERYDAY SOUNDS can grab our attention and bring us into the present. When we hear them, we answer the door, turn off the stove, check our schedule, or sometimes grimace at an unwanted intrusion. But we can also *use* such interruptions as "mindfulness bells" that help us to bring our awareness to exactly where we are. Each moment we are in the present is an opportunity to cultivate awareness. There are many kinds of mindfulness bells in our world. At first, we may decide to pause for reflection only when a "real bell" sounds, such as a telephone. Over time, we can begin to use other events in our daily life as cues. Water can become a mindfulness bell, for example, so that each time we wash dishes or bathe we recognize that we are touching the bountiful gift of water, which nourishes all life. Even if we start by recognizing only one "bell," mindfulness can begin to infuse our lives.

May I learn to attend
to all the mindfulness bells
in my world,
so I can be present for my life
and for the blessings
that surround me.

HARMONY

One string on the guitar is irritatingly out of tune.

My coworkers' snide comments disrupted the meeting.

My garden is a soothing place for reflection.

WE CAN DEVELOP HARMONY in our inner world and in the world around us when we ensure that all elements interact pleasantly. But if even one part is out of sync, it can—like a splash of incompatible color in a painting—produce disharmony. Sometimes we can spot incongruity in objects around us and see a "correction" quickly. Disharmony in our hearts and minds is more challenging to notice but often is perceived as discomfort, obsession, or aversion. It is critical to our spiritual tranquillity that we restore inner balance through a daily spiritual practice such as meditation.

May I work
with mindful awareness
toward inner and outer harmony
that I may live peacefully
and help generate accord
among others.

SPIRITUAL EFFORT

My friends are sharing stories about someone not present, and I consciously avoid contributing to the gossip.

I know I should telephone my father, but I have to force myself to make the call today.

I am working so hard as a volunteer that I am totally exhausted.

WHEN WE UNDERSTAND that our spiritual goal is to lead a life of nonharming, we can exert just the right amount of effort—neither too much nor too little—to restrain ourselves from taking actions harmful to ourselves, others, or the world. With this effort, we generate the energy we need for beneficial deeds. This balance of effort creates the energy that sustains our journey on the Middle Path, a spiritual passage that avoids extremes.

May I be willing
to mindfully cultivate the effort
I need to pursue spiritual growth
on the Middle Path.

RENUNCIATION

Sometimes I think I should throw it all away and join a monastery.

Sometimes I seem to live in my head.

Sometimes I welcome my justified anger.

WHEN WE HEAR THE WORD *renunciation*, we may think it means to give up everything we take pleasure in and live a life of asceticism. But true renunciation involves rejecting any thought, intention, word, or action that causes suffering to ourselves and others. It sometimes seems easier to understand why we would refrain from harmful words and actions than it is to shun harmful thoughts and emotions. Especially those of us who have habitually lived in our heads find it challenging to eschew the stories our minds invent as insubstantial ephemera that can manifest as unskillful intentions. And no matter how "noble" or "justified" our negative emotions may seem, we must acknowledge that indulging them merely plants the karmic seeds for later pain.

May I live always
in the present moment
with the wisdom
and the mindful awareness
to renounce my harmful thoughts
as they arise
and my harmful words and actions
before they occur.

AGING

I still feel so young, but…

Putting on my shoes, I notice that the skin on my knees seems to have been replaced by crepe paper.

Walking down the street, I pass unnoticed by the types of people who used to follow me with their eyes.

My hands can't open the "childproof" bottles of medicine for my arthritis.

I put on my glasses—not just to read the telephone book, but to eat dinner.

EXPERIENCES LIKE THIS can make us feel excluded by Western culture, which glorifies youthfulness and emphasizes sports and other activities possible for only the young and able-bodied. Yet the signs of aging that people here spend millions of dollars trying to conceal are respected symbols indicating wisdom and experience among other cultures. When we focus on only the external indications of aging, we forget the internal treasures that we accumulate with each year of our lives.

Each day,
may I view my life
as a process and mindfully embrace
the markers of aging
that manifest at every stage.

ILLNESS

This cold is making me miserable.

As I age, I feel as if the warranty on my body parts has run out.

I hope this cough isn't a sign of lung cancer.

WHEN WE BECOME SICK, we often take the illness personally and feel that our happiness is conditional upon getting rid of it. We forget that illness—along with aging and death—is a hallmark of our human existence, and we get angry at our bodies for "letting us down." Sometimes, out of fear, we generate horrendous stories about our illness that may cause us more suffering than the illness itself. When we realize that illness is inescapable, that stress around illness increases our suffering, and that being sick is not a shortcoming, only then can we be at ease with, and even empowered by, illness.

When I experience
the unavoidable illnesses
that are part
of my human condition,
may I be mindful of impermanence,
free from fear,
and grateful for the blessings
that also arise and pass away.

DEATH

My pets will die.

My parents will die.

My friends will die.

I will die.

ENCOUNTERS WITH ILLNESS, old age, and death ignited the spiritual quest of the man who was to become Shakyamuni Buddha, and we too must confront these quintessential instances of impermanence. Though it is certain that we and those we love are not exempt from death, we nevertheless experience great suffering around it. Stunned by each loss, we search for some way to adequately gird our emotions for the inevitable next loss of someone we care for. We can learn much about death by developing awareness of the fleeting "little deaths" that are our everyday experiences as they arise and pass away. With this awareness, we can learn to live today, this moment, as if it were the last day of life for us and our loved ones. When we do this, our priorities shift dramatically, and we can act from a heart space of gratitude and generosity toward all of life.

Acknowledging that
I and everyone I love will die,
may I cherish the blessings
that appear in my life
and those with whom I share them.

PRAYER
AND MEDITATION

Sitting on a cushion, I can meditate.

Kneeling in a church, I can pray.

Sharing coffee with a loved one in the kitchen, I can connect with the sacredness of life.

WE OFTEN THINK we can pray and meditate only if the conditions are "right." Unless we are sitting in a church, sitting in a meditation hall, or taking directions from a guru, spiritual practices may seem quite pointless. Fortunately, we can break through these formalities and transform our lives into a spiritual conversation when we embrace the adage that prayer is speaking and meditation is listening. Formal intensive prayer and meditation have been shown to ease minds and even lower blood pressure. But, for believers of all faiths, special blessings come to us when we learn to informally pray and meditate as we communicate with those we love, for then we speak to all that is universal in them even as we listen with focused attention to universal truth speaking through them to us.

May I find the blessing
of inner silence and peace
that I may mindfully
speak to and listen for
interconnectedness
between myself and others.

MEDITATION
AND REFLECTION

When I meditate first thing in the morning, my days go better.

Practicing yoga helps me feel centered.

Reflecting on spiritual teachings inspires me.

ALTHOUGH SOMETIMES *meditation* and *reflection* are used interchangeably, it is also sometimes valuable to distinguish between the two. In the Buddhist tradition, for instance, meditation is a practice that concentrates the mind and calms the body through focusing on our breath, particular words, visualizations, or movement and is a training practice for cultivating mindful awareness. When we meditate, we gain insight into reality, into just how things are, as well as experience beneficial side effects such as mental peace, reduced stress, lower blood pressure, and stronger concentration in our other activities. When we engage in reflection, we contemplate spiritual wisdom for inspiration, comfort, and guidance in living the kind of life we won't regret.

May I use meditation
to come mindfully into the moment
and through reflection
appreciate the blessings
that fill my life.

BREATH

Filled with anger and fear over a narrowly averted road collision,
I become aware of my rapid, shallow breathing.

I learn of a friend's death and feel heavy pressure on my chest
and tightness in my throat as my breath escapes in sighs.

Waiting for the dentist to begin drilling, my stress level rises;
then I take three deep breaths and the tension dissipates.

BREATH IS LIFE ITSELF moving through our bodies. But unless we consciously pay attention to our breathing, perhaps during meditation, or it changes abruptly in response to external circumstances, we are unaware of our breath. When we are mindful of it, it can tell us much about our emotional state, it can bring us into the present moment, and we can deliberately use it to calm our mind.

Mindfully attending to my breath,
may I be aware of the gift of life
flowing through my body.

KARMA

My family came to the United States seeking religious freedom.

When I got angry at my son, I remembered my father's wrath toward me.

Why do I keep doing the same hurtful things but expect different results?

WE OFTEN HEAR the term *karma* used to mean unavoidable destiny, but the "law of karma" actually refers to the absolutely lawful relationship between *intentional* cause and effect. Everything that has ever happened—whether it was intentional or not—has become part of our karma, and karma is individual, family, even national. Although we cannot change what has happened in the past, we can change *our* future by the choices we make in the present. Our karma will, like fruit, ripen from the thoughts and actions we have planted. But the manifestation, again like seeds, will occur on its own schedule. We can't always know or predict or see the way karma will unfold—it sometimes seems quite mysterious—but it always will.

Although my past karma
cannot be changed
may I be mindfully present
in the moment,
to create karmic seeds of happiness
for myself
and the world.

CAUSE AND EFFECT

"What difference do thoughts make if I don't act on them?
Who would know?"

"Why shouldn't I linger in the shower as long as the
hot water lasts? Who would care?"

"So what if the United States uses a quarter of the world's
resources but has a twentieth of the population. We work hard!"

BY INDULGING NEGATIVE THOUGHTS and selfish impulses, we become increasingly negative and selfish people. The "law of karma" teaches us that no action or intention is ever lost, and there is a direct relationship between our actions and intentions and their results in ourselves and our world. Seeds are a good metaphor for the lawful relationship between cause and effect: What we plant, so shall we reap—if we plant pumpkin seeds, we will not grow asparagus—and the harvest will occur at the time and under the conditions the seeds require in order to ripen. Our deliberate thoughts and actions today are like seeds that will inevitably mature into our actions tomorrow. When we are aware of our intentions in the present, we can shape our future. This inescapable possibility is what makes us free.

Aware that no intention or action
is ever lost,
may I mindfully accept the gift
of being free,
in each moment,
to shape my life
and the world.

HANDS

I plant my garden.

I reach out to steady someone who stumbles.

I prepare and serve a meal.

THERE IS A FAMILIAR SAYING: "My hands are the only hands God has." We can use our hands with awareness to mold our future even as we use them to fulfill our daily tasks and to help others. But our hands also eloquently communicate the continuity of our place in time. When we contemplate them, we can see our past in the lifelong changes of their contours and skin texture. Perhaps our hands are shaped like those of a parent or have the coloration of our grandparents. We see our hands in the small fists of our baby. Our hands hold all of history, as well as all of the future.

Aware
that all who have come before me
and that will come after me
live in my hands,
may I mindfully use my hands
to bring blessings to myself
and others
in the present
and for the future.

PRESENCE
OF HEART

EMOTIONS

Some days I feel unlovable.

I was so angry at him I thought I'd never forgive him.

When I finally had the family I'd always wanted, I thought,
"Now I'll be happy."

WHEN STRONG EMOTIONS ARISE—positive or negative—we think
they will never change or go away. Emotions are real, but they are not
facts: Just because we have the painful feeling of being unlovable does-
n't mean that we are. Emotions are not permanent or absolute; they
arise and change and pass away, as impermanent as everything else.
Especially when difficult emotions come up, we tend to generate stories to justify them, and the stories and emotions feed each other,
like a second arrow we shoot into our original painful wound. When we
can be present for our emotions and can see them for what they are—
impermanent and deceptive—we can integrate reason and emotion
and not be victimized by our feelings.

May I recognize
that even my strongest emotions
are temporary,
and have power over me
for only as long
as I give it to them.

HAPPINESS

A child smiles, and so do I.

A bird sings, and my heart is lighter.

A friend gives me a hug, and I warm with pleasure.

EVERYONE WANTS TO BE HAPPY, but we often forget that we can find happiness only by being present for such precious moments *today,* not by dwelling on what we had yesterday or want for tomorrow. Contentment also evades us when we cling to people, things, and situations as if possessing or controlling them will determine our lasting happiness. But these objects of our desire can never assure enduring happiness because they are fleeting and changeable, and when they change—as all things do—we suffer. We cannot freeze everything in our lives so that nothing changes. A conditional happiness dependent upon any specific circumstances always leads to suffering. Only by being fully present and cultivating gratitude, generosity, and kindness can we find the renewable source of happiness in ourselves in each moment.

Cultivating gratitude,
generosity, and kindness,
may I be fully present
for the many blessings in my life
so I may know happiness
through my gratitude
for even the smallest wonders.

GRIEF

A loved one dies—a parent, a child, a friend, a pet—
and I am flooded by an unexpectedly shocking wave of grief.
No matter how deeply I thought I knew that death and loss are
inevitably part of the impermanence of life, <u>this</u> death, now,
catches me completely off-guard and is astonishing.

WE SOMETIMES FEEL that few others can ever have experienced pain
as penetrating as our own grief, but all around us newspapers, maga-
zines, films, and television programs are filled with images that mirror
our sorrow. The life situations of the mourners we see depicted often
are very different from ours. But when we witness the anguish of a
mother cradling the body of a child who has starved to death, the
despair of a child at a parent's burial, or the wretchedness of a person whose family has been killed in a natural disaster or wartime
tragedy, we see clearly that their suffering is very much like ours. Few
experiences teach us about impermanence as compellingly as does
the death of a loved one. When we can truly acknowledge the reality
of impermanence in the face of death, the universality of emotions
such as grief can bring us comfort even as it enhances our awareness
of our interconnectedness with all other beings.

Recognizing that everything in life
is impermanent, may I recall
the universality of suffering
and take mindful solace
within the community of all beings.
Even as I mourn what I have lost,
may I be present in <u>this</u> moment,
grateful for all I have.

SUFFERING AND PAIN

Why is there so much suffering in the world?

My aging knees howl with pain every time I climb stairs.

While one California county diverts water to keep golf courses green, the crops farther downstream are parched and farmers are going bankrupt.

THERE ARE TWO BROAD CATEGORIES OF SUFFERING. The first, pain, is inevitable, but much of other suffering is optional. We cannot avoid the pain of aging, illness, and death. But if we make our happiness dependent upon things and people we are attached to, we will eventually add "optional" suffering to our human condition because all things—and people—are impermanent. We create much of this kind of suffering through the stories we tell ourselves about what we believe will bring us happiness. Whenever we crave for things—health, sense experiences, people, possessions—to be different than they are, we create suffering for ourselves. When states or nations fall into the same kind of greed for things like territory, resources, and power to be different, they can create suffering on the scale of catastrophe.

May I face the painful experiences
that are inevitably part of life
with mindfulness
instead of embellishing stories
that increase my suffering.

COMPASSION
AND PITY

When I encounter a panhandler, I usually give him a quarter
because I feel bad for him.

I sometimes become irritated when a driver pulls into
the last available parking space, even if it's one reserved
for handicapped people.

WE ARE SURROUNDED BY PEOPLE challenged by distress, sometimes as inconsequential as frustration over a traffic delay, sometimes
as devastating as the loss of their home, health, livelihood, or a loved
one. How we respond to the pain of others depends upon the openness of our heart. No matter how sad we may feel, when we pity others we perceive ourselves as inherently separate from and even above
them because they are having emotions or problems that we do not
share. But we can respond with genuine compassion when we can
acknowledge and empathetically identify with their emotions. We can
give them comfort because we can share their pain without having to
fix it for them. Pity often resembles compassion, but it comes from a
very different heart space.

May I mindfully meet
the suffering of others
with the grace of an open heart
so that I may
compassionately share with them
the emotions
natural to our human condition.

GUILT AND REMORSE

I'm embarrassed to say so, but I wanted the job so badly
that I was willing to say anything to get it.

It's painful to look back over the missed opportunities of my youth.

I feel so bad about the scene I caused at my family's reunion.

I should have spent more time with my mother before she died.

WE DO NOT HAVE TO HAVE COMMITTED A CRIME or some repre-
hensible act in order to feel guilt. There are many instances in our
everyday life that can cause us remorse, sometimes because of something we've done, other times because of something we didn't do.
The singular characteristic of guilt and remorse is that we feel them for
something that happened earlier in our lives. Because there's no way
to rewrite the past, guilt is a purely negative emotion unless we use it
as motivation to learn and change so that we act more responsibly in
the present.

Mindfully letting go of guilt
and remorse,
may I draw on experiences
of the past
to shape a present
that will cause
neither guilt nor remorse
in the future.

SYMPATHETIC JOY

When a baby grins at me, I feel as if my heart will burst
open with joy.

I look at the bride and groom's smiling faces and ruefully think,
"You just wait."

I hear myself ask, "How come she's so happy?"

I've succeeded in my career but still I wonder, "Is this all there is?"

BABIES' SMILES, kind words, a beautiful sunset, a brilliant accomplishment—many things, large and small, can unleash waves of happiness in us. But the exuberant joy of others can sometimes elicit from us such negative feelings as envy, jealousy, and judgmentalism. When we encounter the seeming unbridled happiness of others, we may get caught up in comparing our quotient of joy to theirs. We may imagine that joy is somehow a finite quantity and that if someone else has a lot, we'll have less. Occasionally it is difficult for us to take joy in even our own achievements if we do not value ourselves and appreciate what we have attained.

May I mindfully cultivate
gratitude
for all the blessings in my life
so that I may take delight
in others' successes
as well as my own.

AVERSION

I disliked that doctor so much I couldn't wait to get
out of her office.

How can my nephews listen to that dreadful noise they call music?

I hate waiting in lines.

WE EXPERIENCE AVERSION whenever we reject something because
we deem it unpleasant—a person, a situation, a mental or physical
experience. We may not recognize aversion when it takes such forms
as ill will, hatred, jealousy, envy, and judgmentalism because it seems
so reasonable, so justified. But whenever we are caught up in aversion,
our equanimity is thrown off balance, and aversion makes it impossi-
ble for us to see the truth and experience liberation in this moment.
Every experience of aversion is an opportunity for spiritual growth if
we can separate the cause of the aversion from our response to it and
see and acknowledge the way things really are.

Mindfully recognizing
the destructiveness of aversion,
may I let go of it
each time it arises,
and take advantage
of the opportunity it gives me
for insight, wisdom,
and spiritual growth.

ANGER

Another driver cuts me off.

My partner leaves dirty dishes in the sink.

My puppy soils the carpet.

EVERYDAY LIFE is filled with little affronts, but sometimes we find ourselves in an ongoing work or family situation that is so stressful we feel angry much of the time. Even under such conditions, rather than identifying ourselves as an "angry person," we can simply acknowledge the fact that anger is present. Like all states of heart-mind, anger is impermanent: It blazes up as the result of a current situation and is extinguished when conditions change. When anger is not present, we may feel contented and cannot even discern its hiding place. The presence of anger in our mind is important to notice before we speak or act in a wrathful manner. Anger often serves to mask fear, and once we realize this and acknowledge fear honestly, anger frequently goes away quickly. "Righteous anger" can teach us much about how we separate ourselves from others even as it alerts us to injustice.

Whenever anger arises,
may I recognize its
transitory nature
and respond with understanding
rather than reacting with wrath.

ENVY AND JEALOUSY

My mother always seemed to favor my sister.

If I had his money I could drive a Land Rover too.

My husband probably persists in working late so he can spend more time with that new secretary.

WHEN THE "GREEN-EYED MONSTER" of jealousy and its companion ogre, envy, raise their heads, we always suffer. Jealousy and envy arise throughout our lives, perhaps beginning as sibling rivalry, and can be especially enraging when we feel that we are being denied something unjustly. The act of comparing what we have to what someone else has makes us miserable, especially whenever we want for ourselves an advantage, a thing, or even the attention of person that we perceive someone else to have. We hold on to our feelings of entitlement, start to generate stories, and increase our unhappiness as we create separation between ourselves and others.

When envy or jealousy arises,
may I mindfully
cut through storytelling
and, letting go of the suffering
these stories generate,
may I see things as they are.

FEAR AND ANXIETY

Losing a job.

Preparing a meal for a large gathering.

Being unable to get health insurance.

Walking down a dark street in a strange city.

Not receiving an expected call from a loved one.

MYRIAD SITUATIONS CAN ELICIT FEAR or its more generalized relative, anxiety. Fear and anxiety are always projections about something in the future, something that has not yet happened. When fear arises for us, we avoid and separate ourselves from its source, sometimes even denying that it exists and masking it with other emotions such as anger. But when we resolutely come into the present moment, we can counter fear through seeing the threat as the projection it is and knowing that everything, including our fear, is impermanent and will pass away just as surely as it has arisen.

May I hold my fear gently,
with compassion for myself,
so that the actuality
of the present moment
can banish it.

PRESENCE OF HEART

DESIRE AND GREED

I long to be a more compassionate person.

I would be totally happy if the love of my life were really mine.

I'll just eat one potato chip.

WHEN WE SEEK QUALITIES such as kindness and compassion, desire can be a positive motivation for spiritual growth. All too often, however, we desire an object, a house, a job, or a person so powerfully that desire becomes greed, and we create for ourselves one of the most potent basic causes of suffering. When we are first caught up in the desire/greed cycle, we can see only what is attractive about the object of our craving. This kind of attachment is based on the assumption that attaining the object of our desire is a sufficient condition for our lasting happiness. But when things change—and they always do—we find ourselves disappointed and unhappy, and we begin to look around for another target for our desire. Desire is insatiable, it sends us on quest after quest, and it leaves us feeling diminished and separated from others and the world.

May I mindfully acknowledge
the impermanence of satisfaction
brought by objects of desire,
letting go of all greed
and cultivating desire only
for experiences that lead me
further along my spiritual path.

PRESENCE
OF MIND

THOUGHTS

Every time I think about what my life would be like if I had
gotten that other job, I feel despondent.

I was so lost in thought that I drove right past my exit.

I thought about all the pros and cons for a long time before
I ended the relationship.

UNCHECKED, our thoughts have tremendous power over us. Painful
thoughts can cause us great suffering, and we can become so caught
up in pleasant thoughts that we may lose contact with such realities
as where we are or what time it is. Ironically, although thoughts have
no substantiality and in fact simply are *nothing other than* thoughts and
may indicate nothing about the world, we speak and act based on
them. In this way we shape our world through our thoughts. When we
recognize thoughts for what they are—and are not—we see that
mindful awareness rather than merely *thinking* can lead us to wisdom
and to a happiness based on what is true.

Acknowledging
that the contents of my thoughts
are not facts,
may I shape my world through
the wisdom of mindful awareness
and insight.

INTENTIONS

I really telephoned him to make him feel guilty for not calling me.

I was just chatting away—I never meant to hurt her feelings.

When I'm down, I don't watch the local TV news because it fills my mind with negative thoughts.

OUR THOUGHTS AND INTENTIONS always precede our words and actions and are manifest in them. When we live in the present moment, we can be aware of our intentions and can see their causal relationship with our words and actions. If we welcome and indulge negative thoughts toward others, we will eventually express them in ways that are unskillful. But when we cultivate positive intentions, we develop the kindness and goodwill that can make us happy people who live in equanimity with others. By acknowledging our intentions and taking responsibility for them, we have the genuine possibility of transforming ourselves.

By mindfully taking responsibility
for and modifying hurtful
intentions before they
become actions,
may I recognize and remember that
I have the potential
for transformation.

EXPECTATIONS

I gave my mother what I thought was the perfect gift
but she looked so disappointed.

A friend I cherish as family didn't invite me to a gathering I had
looked forward to attending, and I felt hurt and embarrassed.

WHEN WE HAVE DECIDED in advance how someone else is going to feel or act, we have invested a lot of our own sense of self in our expectations. In all areas of life, great and small, we are continuously directing our activities to goals, including spiritual ends such as generosity, but we may get a wake-up call when our efforts fall short: Whenever we experience substantial disappointment, we are attached to expectations of a specific outcome. Indeed we must plan for the future. We must see our objectives clearly and aim for them carefully, but we open ourselves to suffering when we make our happiness dependent on expected outcomes.

May I clearly see my daily
undertakings and long-range goals
and mindfully pursue them
without making my happiness
dependent upon my expectations.

TRUTH AND REALITY

I thought that if I earned more money, all my problems
would be behind me.

In my anger, I believed that she was completely in the wrong.

I sometimes wonder if everything's relative and there aren't
any "truths."

WE MISTAKENLY SUPPOSE that something external such as a job or
a relationship can make us happy forever or that we can see clearly
through a veil of anger. The real "truths" in our world are not just
about lying and exaggerating but also about our encounter with reality. When we walk a spiritual path, we are seeking deeper truths and
we learn that although many things in life *are* relative, we can only
know reality by insight into such immutable truths as impermanence
and the working of cause and effect in our lives.

Without greed, anger, and delusion,
may I perceive moments
of truth,
of enlightenment,
as I mindfully face and see reality.

HUMILITY

I felt personally humiliated when my team lost.

Getting a promotion was just luck, I guess.

I could have gone so far in life if I had gotten the right breaks.

WE MAY CONFUSE THE CONCEPTS *humility* and *humiliation* and feel shame if we experience a failure or minimize our successes in the guise of humility. Other times, we go in the opposite direction and exaggerate our accomplishments to build ourselves up to impress others. But true humility is an accurate evaluation of our strong points and limitations and modest candor in acknowledging them. Such spiritual detachment is possible only through the realization of our humanness and interconnection with all beings. When we receive compliments for an outstanding performance, we are expressing humility by acknowledging them with the simple words "Thank you." Instead of making excuses for times when we have not excelled, we can express real humility by saying, "I did the best I could."

May I have the humility
to mindfully and accurately
assess my strengths
and my weaknesses
so that I may recognize
my spiritual interrelatedness
with all other beings.

DOUBT

I would like to do fast-walking but I don't have enough stamina to take even a short walk.

She asked, "If God really cares about people, how could so many cruel tragedies happen?"

I thought this silent retreat would bring me peace, but it's the wrong practice for me because I'm so gregarious.

WHEN WE ARE IN THE THROES OF DOUBT, we generate stories about how things should be—or are—to justify and sustain it. We generate and sustain doubt with these stories, but in the process, doubt drains our energy, weakens our intentions, and leaves us indecisive and immobilized. When we recognize doubt for what it is—disbelief in things as they are—we can focus firmly on, and take actions to accomplish, the task at hand, whatever it may be. Only then will we be able to let go of our endless stories.

May I see the events in my life
without distortions
so that I can mindfully
let go of my stories
and dispel the doubt
they generate.

IDEAS AND OPINIONS

If Republicans control Congress, I believe this country
will go to hell.

I've never played video games because they're all too violent.

My sister just doesn't care about our family and never
comes home for holidays.

OUR STRONGLY HELD IDEAS AND OPINIONS are determined by what
we've seen and heard and been taught. Some, such as the immoral-
ity of causing harm to others, may be our natural response to reality
itself. But when they are unexamined, we can box ourselves into dog-
matic stances and find ourselves living with decisions we may have
made decades ago that may or may not have justifiable bases. Our
attachment to ideas and opinions is a key source of suffering when
we make our happiness dependent upon the world meeting our cri-
teria for "rightness." Especially with family and friends, we cannot
dictate that they will view our relationships the same way we do and
act accordingly.

May I mindfully examine
my opinions and beliefs
with an open heart
and a clear mind,
so that my happiness does not
depend upon rigid conceptions.

RESTLESSNESS

I was so bored, I felt as if I would jump out of my skin if I didn't get up and walk around for a while.

Instead of going to sleep, I just kept going over and over what route I would take to the airport the next day.

I worried about every possible detail of our vacation, and a few that weren't possible at all.

A MAJOR DISTRACTION in everyday life—and a hindrance to peaceful meditation—is restlessness: physical, mental, sometimes both. Physical restlessness is so uncomfortable that we tend to spot it quickly, but we can become quite lost in mental restlessness when it takes the form of compulsive planning, obsessive worrying, or "monkey mind," almost always about the future. When we become aware of restlessness, we can short-circuit the stories that fuel it and relax into awareness of our breath, in the moment.

Acknowledging that they dissipate
my energy and my focus,
may I let go of mental
and physical restlessness
and come into mindfulness
of just this moment.

CONCENTRATION

Fully absorbed in the novel I'm reading, I don't notice when people come and go around me. I don't think about something that happened yesterday or might come up tomorrow. I am calm and attentive to every nuance in the book's story.

WE EXPERIENCE moments of intense concentration in many situations—watching an exciting sports event or a good movie on television, working on an art project, or listening to music. Meditation practice can help us to develop this kind of concentration accompanied by mindfulness, which we can bring to the tasks of everyday life. When we really pay attention to our world, we are happier and more effective, because we are fully in the present, tranquil, and mindfully aware of what we are doing.

Through meditative practice,
may I increase the powers
of concentration
that will bring me mindfully
and peacefully into
the present.

PRESENCE
OF CONDUCT

MOTIVATION

I read so many self-help books to try to be happy.

I studied hard so that I would be successful.

I took a job because of the high salary.

I got into a relationship hoping to live "happily ever after."

EVEN WHEN WE DON'T CONSCIOUSLY ADMIT IT, an underlying motivation for all our actions as human beings is the simple fact that we all want to be happy. All too often, however, we make our happiness conditional on achievements, material possessions, and relationships. Because everything we grasp as "the thing that will make us happy" is subject to change, we are doomed, sooner or later, to dissatisfaction or downright unhappiness. Only when we recognize how temporary such solutions are can we make a commitment to altruistically following a spiritual path that can bring lasting happiness to others as well as ourselves.

Acknowledging
the universal desire
for happiness,
may I cultivate the
openheartedness
to mindfully dedicate the blessings
that come into my life
for the benefit of others
as well as myself.

ETHICAL ACTIONS

Buying a car, I choose a practical, reliable vehicle rather than
the appealing one that gets lower gas mileage.

Despite the deadline to finish a project, I listen carefully
and caringly to a friend who needs to share his grief.

In setting up a retirement plan, I invest in a "socially responsible"
fund rather than another one that pays higher dividends but
includes mostly companies that exploit their workers.

ALL THE WORLD'S RELIGIONS have commandments or guidelines
that help us to live together on this planet without harming others
through our thoughts, words, and deeds. But ethical actions do not
consist only of prohibitions. In our daily lives, in our speech and
actions, for every "Don't," there's a positive "Do" that is equally critical. When we take advantage of opportunities to help as well as merely
avoiding actions that cause manifest harm, we enhance our potential
for spiritual growth.

May I embrace mindful
commitment to actions
that help and do not harm,
creating a safe world
for those around me
even as I make possible
my own spiritual transformation.

HARMFUL ACTS

The raging driver cursed at me and nearly rammed my car
when I tried to merge from the ramp.

A parent yells at her child in a supermarket.

A corporation is careless about its greenhouse emissions.

WE DON'T HAVE TO GO INTO WAR ZONES to witness harmful
acts—we are surrounded by deeds small and large that hurt others.
At some time in our lives, we all act in ways that harm others because
we are not happy, not accepting the reality of how things are; we are
suffering, perhaps from fear or greed. The simple rule is that truly
happy people do not intentionally hurt others. When someone harms
us, if we can create conditions for happiness rather than violence, we
break the cycle that perpetuates harming.

May I, through mindfulness,
compassion, and kindness
toward those who create suffering,
help generate conditions
of happiness for those
who cause harm to other beings.

DISCIPLINE

I practice scales so I can play music with others.

I hit tennis balls against a wall so I can better compete
in a tournament.

I save money for a vacation.

I meditate to improve mindfulness and concentration
in my everyday life.

WHENEVER we fruitfully discipline our bodies and our minds, we do so not because self-control is an end in itself. Rather, we maintain disciplinary practices to bring greater pleasure and accomplishment for our real goal: life outside the sphere of restraint.

May I willingly practice
mental and physical disciplines
that will lead to greater freedom,
skill, and joy in my everyday life.

SPEECH

One neighbor whispers that another is a miser.

A minister implores her congregation to help a family in need.

Politicians always seem to insinuate that their opponents
are dishonest.

Children play Telephone and are surprised
by how much the meaning of a simple sentence
can be distorted in retelling.

WE DON'T HAVE TO SEE scratchy old films of Hitler haranguing followers to commit atrocities or of Gandhi pleading for peace to see clearly the power of the spoken word. There are examples all around us of how the human ability to communicate through speech is both a great blessing and a dreadful bane. We can use language to soothe or to provoke others. We can express the truth or obscure it. We can praise others or build ourselves up at others' expense. We can articulate ideas of significance or fritter away time with gossip and frivolous words. We can speak when we should be silent and remain silent when we should speak out. How we speak, consciously or unconsciously, can bring either unrestrained joy or persistent sorrow to those around us and to ourselves.

May I always mindfully speak
words that are true,
useful, and timely,
using wise speech
to bring comfort, respect,
and understanding
to others.

EXAGGERATION

He repeatedly complains that he's the most unhappy person
in the world.

In important social situations, I seem to enhance the image
I present of my position or family background or lifestyle.

With friends, I tend to relate a story with much more drama
than the original situation warranted.

WE OFTEN DISTORT THE TRUTH to build up ourselves or something
or someone we care about. Exaggerations fuel our sense of difference
and separateness—of Self and Other. If we accept people and things
for who and what they are, we have no need to try to convince others that they are better than they are. Exaggeration is a reflection of
insecurity or a rejection of reality, even when it takes the seemingly
harmless form of embellishments to make a story—or ourselves—
seem better or more entertaining. When such doubt of our own and
others' intrinsic merit pervades our lives, exaggerating becomes a
habit-forming kind of dishonesty that may seem to reinforce our
esteem even as it is eroding it.

May I always know
that what is real
is good enough
so I may appreciate
the gifts I have
for just what they are.

PRESENCE OF CONDUCT

GOSSIP

I worked with a bunch of fools—no one else in my office knew what they were doing.

After I left the party, I really regretted telling that story about my neighbor even though everyone laughed.

I think he's got the morality of a hedgehog, don't you?

WHEN WE GOSSIP, we talk negatively about someone who is not present, and it affects both us and them badly. Sometimes we gossip to build ourselves up at others' expense, sometimes to be entertaining or to relieve boredom. Gossiping fuels a judging mind in us, and we use it to bring others into our limiting critical space or to join them in theirs. Gossip can never bring a sense of our connectedness with each other but can only bring separation and disharmony.

May I mindfully use
the gift of speech
for communicating with kindness,
rather than for building myself up
by disparaging others.

INDIFFERENCE

Why should I send money to help people halfway
around the world?

There are so many panhandlers here that I don't even
see them any more.

I don't care enough about this election to stand
in the voting line a long time.

What I do with my life is my business.

WHEN WE ARE HABITUALLY INDIFFERENT to people we don't know,
we gradually close down our hearts, become apathetic toward even
those closest to us, and eventually sever our connectedness with all
beings. Being lukewarm to what happens to other people quickly
becomes harmful negligence, and separating ourselves from people
through apathy can easily lead to indifference in many other spheres
of our lives. When we are indifferent to the institutions that make our
country function, we are accomplices of those who would subvert
them. When we are indifferent to love and kindness, we open the gate
for hatred and irreverence to enter our lives. When we are indifferent
to the suffering of others, we tacitly allow it to continue.

Mindfully aware
that my actions and inactions
affect the whole world,
may I never be indifferent
to the welfare of others
but rather open my heart
to the universal caring
that connects us all.

BALANCE

Exercising strenuously, I drink water and my body regains
equilibrium of fluids and temperature.

After working long hours on a complex project, I go to the movies
to unwind mentally.

I get on a friend's bicycle after many years and pedal
down the lane easily.

AS CHILDREN learning to ride a bicycle, we list and wobble until the enchanted day when we "get it" and ride steadily and calmly down the sidewalk. Life doesn't give us training wheels when we are seeking stability in our daily existence. But, as when we learned to ride a bicycle, once we get the feeling of steadiness, we never lose the possibility. We must be aware in the moment and effortfully strive for balance so that we can experience well-being both physically and mentally.

May I mindfully avoid extremes
of mental and physical stress
so I may realize the balance
of mind and body
that brings peace and happiness.

PRESENCE OF CONDUCT

MODERATION

I ate so much, I fell asleep right after dinner.

At parties, I'm always right next to the chips and dip.

I didn't even eat any of my own birthday cake for fear
that I would gain weight.

IF WE LOOK at our behavior around food, we can often see the ways that overindulgence or asceticism throws us out of our natural balance. Excessive self-indulgence in sensual pleasures fuels craving and greed. It dulls our ability to be fully present for our lives even as it sets the stage for us to take more than our fair share—of food, of material possessions, of shared natural resources. In contrast, excessive asceticism creates emotional contraction and a kind of denial that erodes our esteem while at the same time making us resentful. Moderation is a conscious choice in situations where we have alternatives, and we choose it so that we can maintain balance in our lives.

Avoiding extremes,
may I mindfully choose moderation
in all aspects of my life
so I can maintain the balance that
supports spiritual transformation.

INTEGRITY

The politicians make promises at election time, then renege on them.

Today I told a little white lie—but there's nothing so wrong with that.

If he only wants one song off an album, he'll just get
a pirated track from the Internet.

She acted ethically even though her boss pressured
her to sign false papers.

I know my friends will always tell me the truth.

IT SOMETIMES SEEMS as if the world conspires to erode our ability
to maintain integrity. In public life and private, we are surrounded
by people who model ethical leniency. But when we indulge in even
the smallest moral compromises, we begin to diminish our integrity.
If we can clearly distinguish between actions that harm and those
that do not, and if we can consistently act according to principles
of nonharming, we will have the integrity that is basic to our ability to be a good citizen, parent, spouse, friend, and person.

In large matters
and small details alike,
may I always remain true
to my deepest principles
so that my integrity
can be a gift to others.

LIVELIHOOD

I wake up. I get out of bed. I dress and eat. I lose an hour in traffic. I spend most of the day earning my living. At day's end, I try to unwind, then go to sleep so I'll be rested for the next day's work.

There is so much backstabbing at work because people are afraid of losing their jobs.

I just discovered that there's a tobacco company in my 401k.

WHETHER OUR LIVELIHOOD is as a homemaker or construction worker or executive, we spend most of our waking hours in some way related to earning a living, so our work is the most extensive opportunity we have for spiritual practice. We can't all formally be in the "helping professions," but every choice we make about how we earn our living has a compelling potential for helping the people around us and our environment itself. We can choose a livelihood that is ethical and does not harm others. We can treat our coworkers, clients, underlings, and bosses with respect and kindness. We can use the money we earn to meet our financial responsibilities and to help others. We can use our chosen career to create a caring community in our own home, in the workplace, and in the world at large.

As I meet my financial needs,
may I mindfully make
my source of livelihood
beneficial to my world community
and to those near me.

WORK

I'm a workaholic.

I can't imagine ever doing any other kind of work.

He told me that the only reason he works at all is to pay his bills,
so it didn't matter what he did as long as it brought in the dollars.

IT'S EASY TO SLIP into the pattern of identifying with our jobs so
much that we seem to *be* our jobs. Whenever this happens, we are
creating a sense of Self and Other just as surely as we do when we
buy the currently most fashionable gas-guzzling car to build up
our egos. We are no more what we do than we are what we have.
At the other extreme, we can create an equally compelling sense of
Self and Other by seeing work only as a source of income with no
consideration of whether it contributes to our community or even
whether what we do causes harm to others. Because of its impact
on those around us, our work must always be an integral part of our
spiritual practice.

May I mindfully recognize
my work as an opportunity
to extend my spiritual practice
even as I am fulfilling
my obligations.

LAZINESS AND PROCRASTINATION

I'll clean the house when it really needs it.

I'll make a New Year's resolution to go on a diet.

I'll get a mammogram soon.

I'll finish my degree when I have more time.

WHEN WE ARE FACING AN UNPLEASANT TASK, we can find a multitude of reasons to put it off. Sometimes our laziness takes the form of sluggishness and lack of interest and may be little more than an inconvenience to ourselves or others. But other times there is an underlying fear, and the delay may have grave consequences—as when we procrastinate over taking care of ourselves physically and put ourselves at risk for serious illness. The great tragedy of procrastination is that it truly is a "thief of time," and as we consign our tasks to a mythical future, we waste time, ability, and opportunities.

May I be aware of my laziness
and procrastination
and bring forth timely energy
to do what needs to be done.

STEALING

Because I was prematurely gray, I could easily have gotten
senior citizen discounts even in my fifties.

There's nothing I would enjoy more than taking a long,
hot shower at the end of the day.

My prerogative as a parent is to tell my children what to do
no matter how old they are.

THERE ARE MANY KINDS OF THIEVERY. Whether we are stealing
time or money, taking more than our fair share of resources, or dis-
empowering our children or coworkers, we are violating the precepts
against stealing by taking what is not freely given. Such dishonest or
exploitative theft creates separation between ourselves and others,
strays widely from the moderation that is the Middle Way, and feeds
the selfish desire that underlies suffering. When we are not caught up
in craving, there is space in our hearts for generosity.

May I never take
what is not freely given,
but always give generously
of all that connects me with others.

PRESENCE OF CONDUCT

MISUSING
INTOXICANTS

My parents always have wine with dinner.

He is so boring and insensitive when he's had too much to drink.

She said she didn't remember anything after she left the party.

MANY PEOPLE HAVE A SOCIAL DRINK with dinner and seem to suffer no ill effects. Alcohol in itself is neither good nor bad, but some people are prey to the old Japanese saying "The man takes a drink, then the drink takes a drink, then the drink takes the man." In such cases misuse plays a major role in domestic violence, fatal automobile accidents, and many other kinds of tragedy. Intoxication might happen once by accident, but we would be literally crazy to put ourselves at the same risk time after time and expect different outcomes. Repeated substance misuse is an intentional decision to bring the mind out of balance, and it blurs our ability to tell right from wrong. When we avoid misusing intoxicants, we are heedful of our intentions, words, and actions in ways that cause no harm.

May I be grateful enough for the
blessings of mindful awareness
that I do not excessively use
any intoxicant to blunt it.

FREEDOM

I now have freedom to travel anywhere I like.

When I stopped smoking, I finally gained freedom from that awful addiction.

My family was among the wave after wave of immigrants who came here seeking religious freedom.

I don't feel free to use more than my fair share of the resources.

FREEDOM ALLOWS US to go where we want, act without being driven by compulsion, and live independently without coercion. Freedom may be freedom *to* or freedom *from*, but freedom always means that we have the possibility of choices in our life. However, because the past has determined where we are now, we can have freedom for choices only when we are fully in this moment and understand that reality exists *only now*, fleetingly and ever-changingly. This knowledge gives us *true* freedom to shape our present and our future.

May I mindfully embrace
the freedom to make choices
that living in the moment
affords me.

PRESENCE
IN RELATIONSHIP

FRIENDSHIP

When grief fills my heart, I turn to my beloved friends for comfort.

When life gives me a marvelous gift, I share my joy
with my friends.

When I go to a funny movie, I want to laugh with friends.

FRIENDS ARE THERE WHEN WE NEED THEM TO BE. As youngsters, we may have had many "best friends," but as we grow older, our circle of friends becomes a smaller community of equals who are loyal, generous, loving, and tolerant with each other. An old expression says that love is blind but friendship closes its eyes. Friends give mutual and unconditional support even as we meet our obligation to offer each other constructive comments. Friends give and receive the special kind of love that pays full attention to each other.

May I have mindful appreciation
for the support and company
of my friends,
and may I return
their love and loyalty
as fully and freely
as they bestow them on me.

BEARING WITNESS

I smile as I exchange glances with a man whose daughter has just
taken her first steps alone.

I grieve silently before a memorial to people who have been
killed in war.

I hold my failing mother's hand, sharing a moment with
the caregiver who feeds her sips of water.

I meet the panhandler's eyes as I give her a quarter,
and she murmurs, "Bless you," as much for the authentic
contact as for the coin.

LIFE IS FILLED WITH OPPORTUNITIES for bearing witness to the positive and negative experiences in our world. When we do not turn away from what brings pain *or* what brings happiness, we acknowledge that both always exist—even in the same instant. When we can fully open ourselves to all the delights and challenges to which we and others are heir, without picking and choosing which ones we will attend, we can be part of the tapestry of life around us. Open to both painful and joyful events, we see our interconnection to everything around us even as we recognize that sometimes the only role we can play is to bear witness.

With an open heart, may I bear
witness to all of life's joy
and suffering,
that I may share the gift
of sympathetic joy for others'
happiness and compassion
for their sorrow.

SELF

The song says "I gotta be me," but who or what is that?

Sometimes I feel so different from everyone else.

My parents taught me to depend only on myself, not on others.

WITH MINDFUL OBSERVATION, we can discern that our physical bodies, feelings, perceptions, mental formations, and consciousness are impermanent and come together under specific conditions to create "me"—just as certain conditions of light and atmosphere come to together to create what appears as a rainbow to an observer. When those conditions change, what we call "*me*" disappears, just as a rainbow does. But even as we grapple with the truth of this concept, we can perceive several of its consequences: It is our minds that create dualities such as Self and Other; the stories we tell ourselves reinforce our sense of self; and whenever we make our happiness dependent on that sense of self, we always suffer.

May I break down the separation
my mind creates between
Self and Other
so that I may truly recognize my
interconnection with all beings.

PRAISE AND BLAME

Describing the same event, one colleague loudly gives me credit
for success but another roundly blames me for failure.

My bosses praise me when the company is doing well but blame
me when sales fall off.

I take credit when everything is going well in my life but blame
the politicians when economic conditions seem threatening.

WE ARE ALL SUBJECT TO PRAISE AND BLAME in almost every area
of life—and we subject others to our own praise and blame as well.
Praise and blame may seem to be opposites, but they in no way balance each other. Rather, both can function to separate us from other
people. Praising others with an open heart is an affirming experience,
but doing so with envy causes us spiritual contraction. When others'
praise brings us confidence, it's nourishing, but when it evokes self-sat-
isfaction, it distances us from others. Blame never has positive effects.
Being the object of blame can elicit doubt and insecurity. But most
destructive is blaming others, for it always separates us from them,
even as it disempowers us because we are putting them in control of
our emotions rather than taking responsibility for them ourselves.

With full awareness,
may I give and receive praise
openheartedly
but always renounce the blame
that separates me
from others
and contracts my heart.

COMPARISONS

I enter an unfamiliar social situation and am struck by how at ease, outgoing, and cheerful everyone else seems to be.

I attend a spiritual retreat and everyone around me appears more serene and blissful than I feel.

WHENEVER WE COMPARE our "insides" to other people's "outsides," we are setting ourselves up for disgruntlement. Ironically, if we could somehow observe the thoughts of those others who seem so much more comfortable, we'd find that they are not very different from our own. In making any comparison at all, even of external factors, we court the risk of feeling either superior to them because of what we have and are, or inferior to them because of what we lack—but in every instance, such comparisons separate us from one another. Only when we recognize our commonalities rather than focusing on what we perceive as our differences do we join the human race.

May I identify with others
rather than compare myself
to them so I can experience
the grace of our interconnectedness.

LISTENING

Every time I hear a church bell I recall my sister's wedding.

He harps on the same incidents so often that I just tune him out.

The woman seated next to me was such a kindred spirit that we talked the whole flight about intimate family concerns.

HOW MANY OF THE SOUNDS AROUND US do we really hear? A bell, a train whistle, or a song can transport us into a realm of memories that mask the sound in the present. When people tell the same stories repeatedly, we stop listening. When even close friends say something we strongly disagree with, we shift our attention to our own opinion and never really hear theirs. Yet sometimes we are thrown together with strangers on a train or plane with whom we have remarkably candid conversations. We can tell these unfamiliar persons our deepest secrets because we both are in the present moment and are listening without the preconceived stories we bring to so many of our interactions. Only when we can listen without the imprisoning frame of our imagined and remembered stories can we truly communicate with others.

Opening my heart and mind,
may I fully hear
what others would tell me
that I may nourish understanding
and strengthen the connection
between us.

PRESENCE IN RELATIONSHIP

KINDNESS

When I make a mistake, I'm my own harshest critic.

While hurrying to an important appointment, I see an old woman
struggling with an armload of packages, and I know that
if I stop to help her I will be late.

I recycle containers to lessen the stress on the environment.

KINDNESS BEGINS WITH RESPECT FOR OURSELVES. When we are
experiencing difficult emotions, we can hold them in gentleness or
can beat up on ourselves in ways that erode our confidence. Because
kindness breeds kindness, if we are compassionate with ourselves, we
are likely to take time for acts of kindness toward others and even the
environment. And when we can make kindness the basis of our daily
spiritual practice, we can contribute serenity, compassion, and happiness to our complex world.

May I mindfully cultivate
compassion and understanding
for myself
so that through kindness
I can add happiness, not pain,
to the lives of others.

FORGIVENESS

I thought I could never forgive her for her appalling words.

Can you forgive me for my insensitivity in that moment?

I find it so hard to forgive myself when I've hurt another person.

IF WE DO NOT FORGIVE someone who has harmed us, we experience anger, ill will, and the desire for vengeance. Held onto, these feelings cause us only suffering: We feel stress, have trouble sleeping, lose our appetite, or experience a host of other difficulties, while the person who has offended us goes along blithely unaware of our suffering. If we do not forgive others who have hurt us or even ourselves for harming ourselves in some way, we are not directly facing our humanity, and theirs—not recognizing that we all are not perfect but make mistakes that are sometimes very hurtful. Whenever we withhold forgiveness—no matter what the circumstances—we are contracting our hearts and fashioning a barrier to opening to love. If we separate ourselves from others through nonforgiving, we become immobilized on our spiritual path.

May I mindfully acknowledge
that others, like myself,
are still growing spiritually,
and forgive their past offenses,
as I forgive my own,
so that I can know
the blessing of a loving heart.

LOVE AND LUST

Our affair was wonderful while it was secret.

I thought, "This time, with me, he'll be different."

After we got married, she simply didn't live up to my expectations.

When we sat down to dinner, he picked up the newspaper
and acted as if I wasn't there.

WHEN WE FALL IN LUST and think we've fallen in love, sex is a mood changer and ego booster rather than an expression of the intimate connection that is love. Love—whether between life mates, parents and children, or friends—affirms the loved one for who he or she is. Our love relationships are not about changing another person to fit the ideal of "love" our ego constructs, nor are they about rejecting other persons because, over time, they change, like everything else in life. Love is being truly present with the loyalty, caring, and commitment that confirm the interconnectedness of all beings.

May I mindfully open my heart
in loving acceptance
of those I cherish
and give them the gift
of attentive presence
that strengthens our connectedness.

SEXUAL INTIMACY

Our eyes meet. You smile slightly. I nod with understanding.
You take my hand and we leave the room quickly, impatiently.

IF WE ARE TWO STRANGERS in a bar, the encounter is quite different than when it occurs between a committed and loving couple at home. Whenever and wherever it arises, the sex urge is compelling. Under inappropriate circumstances—for example, in an adulterous affair or any time force is used—this urge can easily be a source of mindless harm, based on ego gratification and selfishness. When we habitually indulge lust as a mood changer, we generate more and more desire, none of which we can ever really satisfy. But when there is mutual commitment between people, desire is transformed into a wonderful aspect of intimacy, and powerful sexual feelings become a spiritual connection expressing affection, love, and deep caring.

May I enjoy
my natural sense desires
in mindful ways
that harm no one
so that sexual intimacy
may always be a blessing
of love and commitment.

HUMOR

When I watched that "comedy," the canned laughter was louder
than even the ads.

"Have you heard the one about the Chinese farmer?"

My favorite T-shirt says, "When did my wild oats
turn to bran flakes?"

IF WE HOOT WITH LAUGHTER only because someone else is bellow-
ing, the humor is probably fairly feeble. When humor produces good-
natured laughter, it is healing and connects us to others because we
are empathetic with the humorist, and the story enables us to see a
situation in a new light that is informative while it is funny. All too
often, however, we hear jokes whose supposed humor relies on malice
toward a particular group: age, race, physical challenge, or nationality. This kind of humor is never healing and separates us from others.
Frequently we are most witty when we affectionately poke fun at ourselves, such as references to our own "senior moments," which are
very different from building ourselves up by taking cheap shots at the
expense of any group or individual.

May I mindfully cherish
moments of gentle laughter
shared with kindness
and find life's humor
through our common foibles
rather than characteristics
that make us different
from each other.

PREJUDICE

"People who talk slowly think slowly."

"Third World countries have primitive culture."

"Middle Easterners hate Americans because they're jealous."

WE HAVE TO BE TAUGHT PREJUDICE. The seeds of discrimination are sometimes planted so deeply, we are not even aware that they are there until something happens and we find ourselves thinking about or acting toward people in a certain way just because of their race, age, nationality, gender, or even regional accent. Often there is no visible evidence for positive or negative biases; sometimes we latch on to incomplete information about things like verbal ability or the notion of what's "primitive." Just as when we first fall in love, we miss reality by seeing only the positive features of our beloved, so too when we feel aversion to a whole group, we perceive only what seems negative. Spiritual practice teaches us how we are like other beings, experiencing and causing pain and joy as we live the lives of change that are our common destiny.

May I be attuned

to the nature of human life,

which is common among all people,

and mindfully use the recognition

of this sameness

to dispel notions of differences

that might make anyone

seem "other."

PETS

My dog sleeps on my bed with ears perked and her head
toward the door so that she can protect me with every ounce
of her ten pounds.

The fish in the aquarium follow my finger as I move it up
and down along the glass.

When I walk in the park, the fearless chickadees land nearby
to see if I have brought them bread crumbs.

THE INTERCONNECTION OF ALL BEINGS is manifest in the curiosity, affection, and communication possible between species who are "aliens" to each other. When we choose to share our lives with animals, we invite into our homes remarkable teachers for our hearts. For the entirety of their lives our pets are as dependent on us for their well-being as babies are. We learn to caringly meet their needs while expecting nothing in return—but they nevertheless give us companionship, loyalty, and unconditional love. In teaching them to do what we expect of them, we become their students: In our devotion to them, we learn from them how to express an unqualified affection—to them, to our loved ones, and to ourselves.

May I openheartedly respect
and love my pets,
learning from them unconditional
love and gratitude
for all beings.

PRESENCE IN THE WORLD

PERSPECTIVE

When I looked at the first NASA pictures from space,
the mountains looked so flat.

I had climbed so high that I was looking down at the clouds.

From a distance, I could spot the pass through the mountains.

MOUNTAINS LOOK COMPLETELY DIFFERENT from various perspectives, and throughout history each view has inspired its own metaphors. When we look up at them, they are the homes of the gods, the symbols of immense size and absolute stability—even though today we know they are slowly and imperceptibly still changing. When we look down from their peaks, we have achieved supreme spiritual goals and overcome the most extreme physical challenge—feeling godlike ourselves because of the miniature world we see. When we look across at them from the valley, we view Nature's most sublimely shaped sculptures, even as we take their measure and decipher their secrets.

May I cultivate in myself
the stability of mountains,
strengthened by the insight
their viewpoints bring.

SEEING

I look out the window at noon and see green trees, yellow flowers, and a brown house. I look out the same window at midnight and perceive only black and gray shapes.

Before changing lanes I check the rear-view and side mirrors but see nothing until I glance over my shoulder and discover another car alongside my rear fender.

When I become angry, I see red. When I am sad, I feel blue.

WE HUMANS rely heavily on our sense of vision, even in metaphors. And yet what and how we see depend upon external conditions such as light and location, upon what we have been taught, and also upon our emotions. All of these conditions determine how we feel about what we see and how we respond through our actions. Whether we find something attractive or aversive does not inhere in the object we see, but rather its pleasant and unpleasant qualities are in "the eyes of the beholder," ourselves.

May I use the gift of vision
to recognize
without discrimination
the ingredients of my world,
mindful that I am imposing
their satisfying and disagreeable
attributes upon them.

EPHEMERAL BEAUTY

I walk barefooted across dawn's chilly dew, sparkling on the grass,
but as the sun rises to light and warm the earth, the glistening
moisture vanishes.

I stare with pleasure at a rainbow arcing brilliantly across the sky,
but when glowering clouds move in and rain begins to fall again,
the rainbow fades away.

I dropped and broke my favorite coffee cup.

WHEN WE ARE ATTENTIVE to dew and rainbows, we are encountering metaphors for all the experiences of our lives, including our lives themselves: When particular conditions occur, phenomena arise—phenomena such as dew and rainbows but also all the events of our lives. When conditions change, as they always do, the happenings that make up our reality fade away just as rainbows do. Just as we do. Only when we acknowledge the certainty of impermanence of even the most mundane objects can we become truly present in the moment.

Acknowledging the truth
of impermanence
may I mindfully enjoy
the ephemeral rainbows of
every moment.

HUMAN NATURE

"Don't blame me for being negative. That's just the way I am."

"Don't mock me for having so many freckles. I was born that way."

"I'm inconsistent because I'm an Aries."

WE ARE A COMBINATION of our genetic heritage, our life history, and the social conditions in which we live. We come into this world with genetic inheritance that gives us a predisposition for certain physical characteristics such as red hair and the potential for mental characteristics such as IQ. We are born with innocence and purity, and during our lifetime our "human nature" is altered by what we learn and what we are taught. We can just let life happen to us or, at any point in our lives, we can take responsibility and transform ourselves into the kind of person we want to be.

May I recognize that when I live
with awareness in the present,
I can change the characteristics
that are barriers to my spiritual
progress.

METAMORPHOSIS

In an early summer ritual, I welcome the monarch butterflies
as they gather after their northern migration to lay their eggs.

I watch in fascination as caterpillars emerge from the eggs
and later spin their cocoons.

Hidden from view, the caterpillars undergo a complete
metamorphosis before they materialize from their cocoons
and unfold their moist wings as butterflies.

THE MONARCH BUTTERFLIES brighten our summer as they gently
brush one plant then another, spreading pollen so that flowers can
happen. Before the first snowfall, we watch monarchs flutter down to
the milkweed in colorful mimicry of the autumn leaves as they begin
their return journey. Migrating south, they bear little resemblance to
the caterpillars of summer. Our metamorphoses too are often internal
and hidden, but they become evident as we go through each stage of
our lives. In every season, we too are learning to become butterflies
and to touch flowers.

Even when my changes
seem slow
or are not visible
may I acknowledge
the possibility of metamorphosis
that is inherent
in my spiritual journey.

PEACE

The politicians say we must make a preemptive assault
to ensure peace.

Saint Francis of Assisi said, "Make me an instrument
of Your peace."

I just want a little peace of mind.

WE MAY FEEL POWERLESS in the face of the large and small hostilities lacerating our planet, but we are not. Peace, both individual and global, begins with us. When we embrace a spiritual path that brings tranquility to our hearts and minds, we are taking the first step toward bringing peace to the world. Inner calmness will create gentle speech and moral actions, and we will replace self-absorption and ill will with a genuine caring for others. As we bring these qualities to communications with our families and friends, people we work with, and those in public life who serve us, we radiate peace out into the world.

May my commitment
to not harming others
through my thoughts, words,
and deeds
inspire me to work
to bring peace to all beings
with whom I share this world.

POLITICS

"Politics is dirty."

"I'm an independent thinker and will never join a political party."

"I don't bother to vote—all those politicians are the same."

IF POLITICS IS DIRTY, it is our responsibility to change it. Only an informed electorate that casts its ballot can ensure that politicians truly govern by the consent of the governed, rather than the few who have the loudest voices or make the largest campaign contributions. In recent decades, fewer than 20 percent of registered voters usually participate in primary elections. When we do not inform ourselves about issues and the differences among candidates, communicate with elected officials, and vote, we have no right to complain about politics. We are part of the problem, because ignorance and apathy are paths of harming.

In mindful gratitude
for such freedom as I have,
may I overcome
ignorance and apathy
and become a force for good.

CONTINUITY

I light one candle on a birthday cake then light six others from it.

I light one candle on the dining room table then light
another from it.

I light one candle on my altar then light two others from it.

WHEN ALL THE CANDLES on the cake are lit, their flames have the same shape. When all the candles on the table are lit, their flames are the same color. When all the candles on the altar are burning, all radiate the same luminosity. The candles are separate from each other, discrete, different. But what about the flames? When one candle is lit from another, don't both burn with the same fire? When we pass the spark of life to a child or the light of inspiration to another, the same flame glows in both of us.

Just as a flame passes
from candle to candle
may mindful compassion
so purely infuse my life
that I can pass it
to all I touch.

EATING

Reading the newspaper while I eat breakfast, I am oblivious
to the oatmeal in my bowl.

The first slice of pie tasted so good that I take another piece
even though I already feel full.

As I wait for my family to come to the dinner table,
my stomach grumbles, my mouth salivates, and I long
to start eating without them.

WHEN WE ARE DISTRACTED by reading, TV, or even conversation, we squander the pleasure that mindful eating creates. When we indulge greed for food, we generate even more craving, overeat, and become drowsy. If, however, we are attentive to sensations of hunger, we can learn a great deal about how desire affects all our daily activities. And when we use eating in moderation as part of our spiritual practice, we develop gratitude for our food and all those beings involved in bringing it to our table.

May I be mindfully present
for the bountiful gift of food
in my life
and at each meal
wish that all beings everywhere
may have enough to eat.

TEACHERS

My parents tell me that I said my first words and took my first
steps before I was a year old.

I found myself repeating a prayer I didn't even know I knew.

When a beautiful bouquet fades, I come face to face
with impermanence.

OUR PARENTS ARE OUR FIRST TEACHERS, guiding us to learn the
basic skills we need in order to adapt to life as human beings. During
our formal education, instructors teach us skills that prepare us for life
as self-sufficient members of society. Our ministers, priests, gurus,
roshis, and lamas are "spiritual midwives" who help us live most fully.
And throughout our lives we are surrounded by bountiful Nature, from
whom we learn the lessons of impermanence.

May I be mindfully present
for life's precious moments
with openness and gratitude so
the whole world can be my teacher.

PRESENCE IN THE WORLD

MUSIC

When I'm happy, I catch myself humming.

When I'm sad, I find comfort in chamber music.

I'm really enjoy chanting at the beginning of my yoga class.

THROUGHOUT HUMAN HISTORY, music has played a vital role. Ancient peoples perceived drums as continuing the sound of our mother's heartbeat before we are born. Others living on savannas had nothing to make instruments of, so they sang. Monastic communities in the East and West chant their deepest beliefs. Through music we express joy, grief, reverence for the sacred. Music enters through one sense with remarkable immediacy and resonates with all the others. With mindfulness, we can cultivate the same closeness through all our senses and interact with all of the world as we do with music.

May the immediacy of music
touch my deepest feelings
and open my heart-mind to the
languages of all my senses.

ART

As I look around my living room, my gaze falls on an African mask, an object I put on the wall and admire as art. But the people who created masks like this one animate them so that they ritually dance in a sacred encounter between spirits and their ancestors. Nearby hangs a Tibetan painting of the life of Buddha, another decoration for my home, but originally an object whose creation through the act of painting—rather than the final image itself—was wholly a spiritual act.

THE QUILTS ON OUR BEDS, the earthenware dishes on our tables, the designs of our computers, even graffiti on the wall down the street— all express the imaginings and ideals of their makers. Even as we perform the most mundane activities of our lives, we are surrounded by objects that reflect the inner life of the people who created them.

May I mindfully acknowledge
the personal expressions of culture
that encircle me,
allowing them
to transcend time and place
and touch my deepest humanity.

SEASONAL CHANGES

Canada geese honk overhead, a shifting V flying south,
sure of their course and certain to return.

Goldfinches flicker their brilliant breeding plumage,
flashing around the feeder like confetti.

A crow hops across the early snow preserved
by cold shadows and leaves a haiku in its path.

CHANGES OF SEASON are marked dramatically by the birds who visit us. Songbirds pipe in spring. Juncos and chickadees flutter down with the first snowfalls. Even when there are fewer birdsongs and fewer winged guests in winter, birds' familiar year-around comings and goings reassure us that there is orderliness in nature's transformation. When we watch them, we know with certainty that we too will play our karmic role in the changing seasons of life.

May I greet the changing seasons
with joy and faith
aware that all is in order,
just as it should be.

177

FIRE

The blazing logs in my woodstove heat my home
on a cold winter night.

The curtain of burning brush moves rapidly up the hillside,
consuming its fuel as it goes.

The glowing burner purifies the compound held in its flame.

ANCIENT PHILOSOPHERS analyzed the four elements of the universe—earth, water, air, and fire—and asserted that these elements are also manifested in human beings. For them, fire was the heat that warms our bodies, caused by the foods we had taken in and were digesting. Later sages found fire an ideal metaphor for emotional states to which we are heir and that can transform us: Love warms the cockles of our hearts. Anger is a conflagration that burns up the fuel that supports it. The fire of faith purifies the heart of the believer. When we look, we can always find fire in our passions, whether we are "angry as hell" or burning with desire.

Mindfully aware of the fires
that inflame my heart
may I use them
to purify my intentions
rather than destroy my equanimity.

DIVERSITY

I pick wildflowers to give as a gift to a loved one.

I put flowers on my altar as an offering to honor
what is sacred to me.

I cast flowers on the coffins of those who have passed on
as declarations of farewell.

FLOWERS OFTEN ACCOMPANY IMPORTANT EVENTS in our lives.
When we gaze at flowers, we encounter an astonishing diversity of
beauty. We find bright red flowers on windblown spikes in the desert
and clustered close to the ground in snowy mountains. We marvel at
them as stunning objects, but flowers did not evolve to satisfy our
aesthetic sensibilities. Rather, their complex petal arrangements and
brilliant colors attract the birds and insects that enable them to repro-
duce and continue their lifecycle. When their purpose is fulfilled, these
glorious flowers fade, wilt, and return to the earth to nourish the diversity of life that comes after them.

May I mindfully appreciate
the diversity
of every being I encounter,
who, like flowers,
brings beauty, variety,
and sustenance
to our world.

THE AIR AROUND US

Acid rain caused by chemical and automotive emissions
has damaged the trees in the mountain forests.

The mayor warned people with respiratory problems to stay
inside today because of the smog.

Many songbirds are disappearing because their habitats
have been destroyed to build highways and malls.

WE ALL ARE BREATHING all the time, though we usually are aware of this life-sustaining process only when it is difficult. One way we can establish a unique awareness of breathing is to go deep into a forest, where we can perceive a freshness in the air that is dramatic testimony to our interrelatedness with all of life. We inhale oxygen produced through the trees' respiration, and we exhale the carbon dioxide that trees require in order to live: We breathe together. Yet whether we are in a forest or our own yard, throughout the natural world we are all "breathing together" in a fragile balance severely strained by pollution of air and water, by destruction of ecological niches, and by creation of chemical, biological, and nuclear waste that could destroy life on this delicate planet. We can no longer embrace the outdated philosophical notion that we must "conquer" nature, for that conquest will kill us and what sustains us.

Mindfully aware
of how I use Earth's resources,
may I cherish
the interrelatedness of all life
and nourish—not merely deplete—
the precious world
that is our home.

ONE WORLD

My uncle had to get a pacemaker because of his heart problems.

Everyone's tears are salty.

When the planes crashed into the World Trade Towers,
something in each one of us died.

BIOLOGICALLY AND GENETICALLY, all life on earth is more alike than different. Emotionally, too, no matter what culture or country we are from, we can be moved by heroic accomplishments and devastating tragedy. It's as if we are living proof of the ancient Vedic myth of King Indra, who had his architects construct a net around the world with a jewel at every junction, so that each jewel reflected and was reflected in every other jewel. Sometimes our lives may have so many loose ends that life seems like a tapestry seen from the wrong side. But when we open our hearts to others, the loose threads in the tapestry of our lives can become woven into Indra's net.

With joy and gratitude,
may I see the beauty of myself
and of others
as we reflect and are reflected
in the radiance of each other—
the sacred web of one world.

ALPHABETICAL LIST OF TOPICS

ALPHABETICAL LIST OF TOPICS

Other useful titles from Wisdom Publications

Meditation for Life
Martine Batchelor
Photographs by Stephen Batchelor
168 pages, ISBN 0-86171-320-8, $22.95

"*Meditation for Life* offers simple, concrete instructions in meditation—and the photographs are delicious eye candy." —*Psychology Today*

The Fine Arts of Relaxation, Concentration, and Meditation
Ancient Skills for Modern Minds
Joel and Michelle Levey
Foreword by Margaret J. Wheatley
304 pages, ISBN 0-86171-349-4, $14.95

"What a beautiful book! It shows the way." —Larry Dossey, M.D., author of *Healing Wounds*

Mindfulness in Plain English
Revised, Expanded Edition
Bhante Henepola Gunaratana
224 pages, ISBN 0-86171-321-4, $14.95

"A masterpiece. I cannot recommend it highly enough."—Jon Kabat-Zinn, author of *Wherever You Go, There You Are*

Mindfulness Yoga
The Awakened Union of Breath,
Body, and Mind
Frank Jude Boccio
Foreword by Georg Feuerstein
320 pages, 100 photos,
ISBN 0-86171-335-4, $19.95

"Editor's Choice!"—*Yoga Journal*

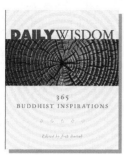

Daily Wisdom
365 Buddhist Inspirations
Edited by Josh Bartok
384 pages, ISBN 0-86171-300-1, $16.95

A spiritual cornucopia that will illuminate and inspire day after day, year after year. Each page, and each new day, reveals another gem of *Daily Wisdom*.

For more information about these and other books from Wisdom Publications, please contact us at:

Wisdom Publications
199 Elm Street
Somerville, Massachusetts 02144 USA
Telephone: (617) 776-7416
Fax: (617) 776-7841
Email: info@wisdompubs.org
www.wisdompubs.org